Ripley® **Readers**

Learning to read. Reading to learn!

LEVEL ONE Sounding It Out Preschool–Kindergarten
For kids who know their alphabet and are starting to sound out words.

learning sight words • beginning reading • sounding out words

LEVEL TWO Reading with Help Preschool Grade 1
For kids who know sight words and are learning to sound out new words.

expanding vocabulary • building confidence • sounding out bigger words

LEVEL THREE Independent Reading Grades 1–3
For kids who are beginning to read on their own.

introducing paragraphs • challenging vocabulary • reading for comprehension

LEVEL FOUR Chapters Grades 2–4
For confident readers who enjoy a mixture of images and story.

reading for learning • more complex content • feeding curiosity

Ripley Readers Designed to help kids build their reading skills and confidence at any level, this program offers a variety of fun, entertaining, and unbelievable topics to interest even the most reluctant readers. With stories and information that will spark their curiosity, each book will motivate them to start and keep reading.

Vice President, Licensing & Publishing Amanda Joiner
Editorial Manager Carrie Bolin

Editor Jordie R. Orlando
Writer Korynn Wible-Freels
Designer Mark Voss
Reprographics Bob Prohaska
Proofreader Rachel Paul

Published by Ripley Publishing 2020

10 9 8 7 6 5 4 3 2 1

Copyright © 2020 Ripley Publishing

ISBN: 978-1-60991-456-1

For more information regarding permission, contact:
VP Licensing & Publishing
Ripley Entertainment Inc.
7576 Kingspointe Parkway, Suite 188
Orlando, Florida 32819

Email: publishing@ripleys.com
www.ripleys.com/books
Manufactured in China in January 2020.

First Printing

Library of Congress Control Number:
2019954291

PUBLISHER'S NOTE
While every effort has been made to verify the accuracy of the entries in this book, the Publisher cannot be held responsible for any errors contained in the work. They would be glad to receive any information from readers.

PHOTO CREDITS

Cover © beboy/Shutterstock **3** © beboy/Shutterstock **4-5** © DLA/Shutterstock **6-7** © Angelo Rocca/Shutterstock **8-9** © Erik Klietsch/Shutterstock **10-11** Science History Images/Alamy Stock Photo **12-13** © Yvonne Baur/Shutterstock **14** © Vadim Sadovski/Shutterstock **15** © Naeblys/Shutterstock **16** © Puslatronik/Shutterstock **18-19** © kyslynskahal/Shutterstock **20** © Ecuadorpostales/Shutterstock **21** © Alberto Masnovo/Shutterstock **22** © Rubi Rodriguez Martinez/Shutterstock **23** © MNStudio/Shutterstock **24** © Aeypix/Shutterstock **25** © aaabbbccc/Shutterstock **26-27** CC BY-SA 4.0 by Astroskiandhike **28** The Asahi Shimbun via Getty Images **29** Doug Perrine/Alamy Stock Photo **30-31** Public Domain {{PD-USGov-NASA}} NASA/JPL **32-33** © LukaKikina/Shutterstock **34-35** © Fransen/Shutterstock **36** © Maksimilian/Shutterstock **37** Nature Picture Library/Alamy Stock Photo **38-39** © Deni_Sugandi/Shutterstock **40-41** © muratart/Shutterstock **40** (b) © Giannis Papanikos/Shutterstock **42** © G Seeger/Shutterstock **43** © Dmitry Kovba/Shutterstock **44-45** © Evdokimov Maxim/Shutterstock **46** (tl) © Pavel Szabo/Shutterstock, (tr) © historiasperiodicas/Shutterstock, (cl) © SDubi/Shutterstock, (cr) © trekandshoot/Shutterstock, (bl) © Fredy Thuerig/Shutterstock, (br) © Alexey Kamenskiy/Shutterstock **47** (tl) © piscari/Shutterstock, (tr) © Hung Chung Chih/Shutterstock, (cl) © mTaira/Shutterstock, (cr) © beboy/Shutterstock, (bl) © ianmitchinson/Shutterstock, (br) David R. Frazier Photolibrary, Inc./Alamy Stock Photo **Master Graphics** © Natutik/Shutterstock, © Shirstok/Shutterstock, © Polina Melnik/Shutterstock, © Nikolai Zaburdaev/Shutterstock

Key: t = top, b = bottom, c = center, l = left, r = right, sp = single page, dp = double page, bkg = background

Ripley Readers

Volcanoes

All true and unbelievable!

Ripley
PUBLISHING
a Jim Pattison Company

TABLE OF CONTENTS

CHAPTER 1
WHAT IS A VOLCANO?

The ground shakes. Smoke fills the air. An explosion is heard from miles away. It's a volcano! Both awesome and fearsome, volcanoes have amazed us for thousands of years!

A volcano is a landform, usually a hill or mountain, that sits above a pool of magma. **Magma** is a very hot type of rock deep below the ground. It is so hot that it flows like a liquid! During an eruption, magma rises through a volcano to the surface of the earth.

Believe *It* or *Not!*

The word *volcano* comes from Vulcan, the Roman god of fire!

A **volcanologist** is a person who studies volcanoes. They research how volcanoes form and what makes them erupt. They also study a volcano's behavior. If they notice anything dangerous, they warn us right away!

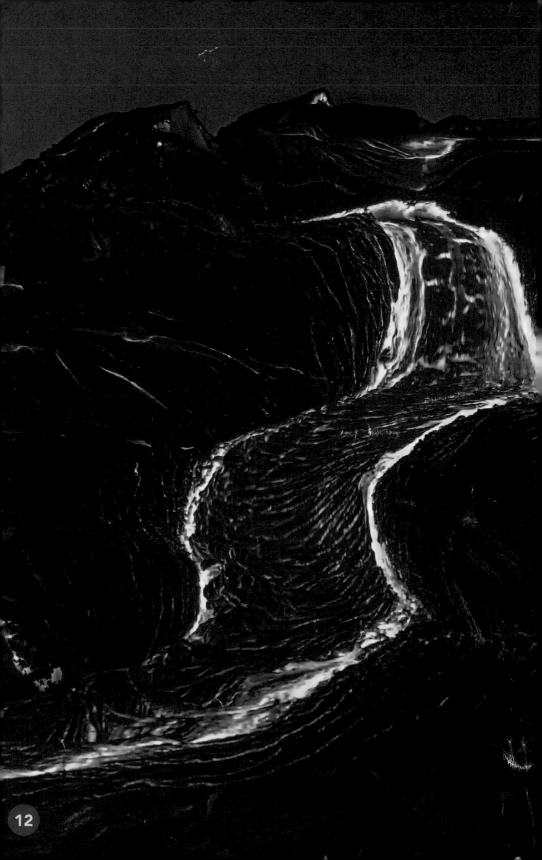

CHAPTER 2
HOW DO VOLCANOES FORM?

Ever wonder how these magma-filled monsters are made? A volcano starts as a crack or vent in the earth's surface where magma can escape.

When magma reaches the earth's surface, it is called **lava**. Lava flows or shoots out of the vent, cools down, and hardens. Together with rock and ash, lava gives a volcano its shape.

To understand volcanoes, we have to understand the earth!

Earth's four layers are the crust, the mantle, the outer core, and the inner core.

Tectonic plates are pieces of Earth's crust that shift around. These plates can move closer, pull apart, or rub together to make a vent. A new volcano is born!

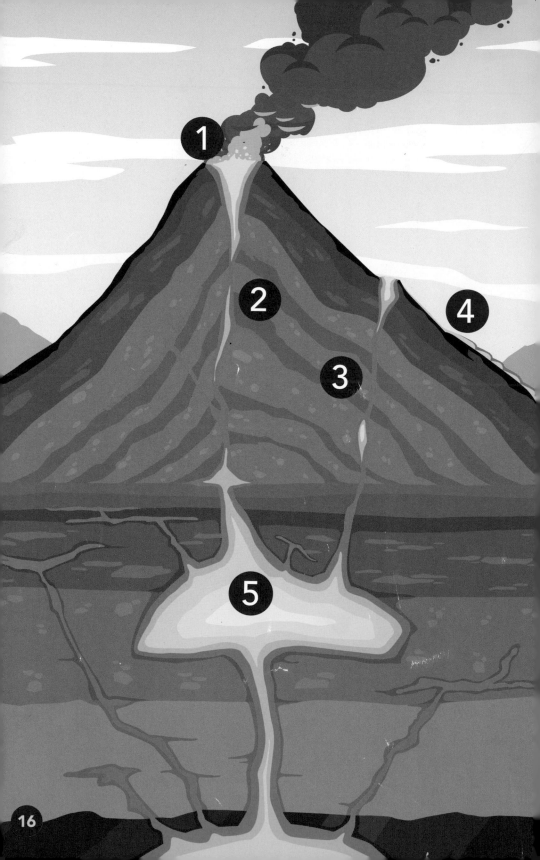

PARTS OF A VOLCANO

1 The *crater* is the bowl-shaped dip on top of a volcano.

2 The *main vent* is the passage in the middle of a volcano where most of the magma escapes.

3 *Side vents* are small passages on the sides of a volcano where more magma can escape.

4 *Lava* is magma that has reached the earth's surface.

5 The *magma chamber* is the pool of hot magma below the volcano.

Believe It or Not! If you think a 90°F summer day is hot, just imagine a magma chamber at 1,200°F degrees!

CHAPTER 3
ALL KINDS OF VOLCANOES!

When you picture a volcano, you probably think of a tall, pointy mountain with lava. The truth is that volcanoes have different shapes, sizes, and ages! Let's take a closer look (but not *too* close—volcanoes are *hot!*).

Volcanoes are either extinct or active.

An extinct volcano is one that hasn't erupted for 10,000 years and is not likely to erupt again.

An active volcano is one that *has* erupted in the last 10,000 years.

A dormant volcano is an active volcano that is not erupting right now but could in the future. There are more than 1,500 active volcanoes in the world!

Believe It or Not! Eruptions are happening as you read this book! Not all of them are loud and explosive. Many are calm and quiet.

A cinder cone volcano shoots lava high into the air. When the lava falls around the vent, it forms a cone shape. These volcanoes do not get very big.

Volcano name: **Parícutin**
Location: **Mexico**
Formation: **1943**
Last eruption: **1952**

Believe It or Not! Do you think you could afford a volcano? Robert Ripley, the father of Ripley's Believe It or Not!, once tried to buy Parícutin!

This gentle giant is a shield volcano. It is the biggest type of volcano but not as explosive as the others. It slowly grows larger over time as lava flows out of its vent. The shield volcano Mauna Loa is the biggest volcano in the world!

Volcano name: **Mauna Loa**
Location: **Hawaii**
Formation: **about 1 million years ago**
Last eruption: **1984**

Volcano name: **Mount Fuji**
Location: **Japan**
Formation: **over 100,000 years ago**
Last eruption: **1707**

A composite volcano is also called a *stratovolcano*. These bad boys can have huge explosions and grow very tall!

Believe It or Not! The tallest composite volcano in the world is Ojos del Salado in Chile. It is 22,615 feet tall!

An eruption is measured on a scale of 0 to 8. The higher the number, the bigger the explosion. **Supervolcanoes** have had a **magnitude** 8 explosion!

Volcano name: **Toba**
Location: **Indonesia**
Formation: **about 1.2 million years ago**
Last eruption: **72,000 BC**

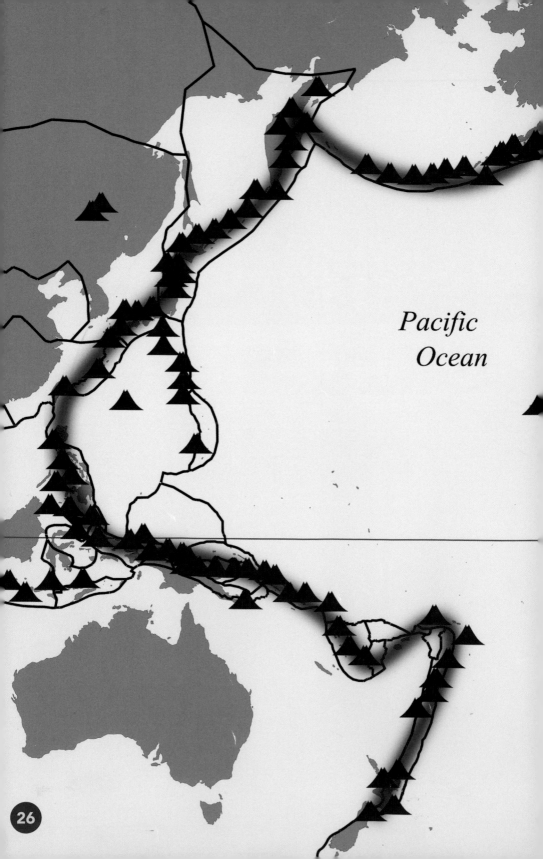

Pacific
Ocean

CHAPTER 4
WHERE ARE VOLCANOES?

Alaska has them. Hawaii has them. Even *oceans* and *other planets* have them! Volcanoes can form wherever tectonic plates are moving.

The Ring of Fire is a path of volcanoes that runs along the Pacific Ocean. There are more than 450 volcanoes along this deadly trail!

Nishinoshima

It may surprise you to learn that most of the world's volcanoes are *underwater!*

These deep-sea sensations can make new islands! Nishinoshima used to be an underwater volcano. After many eruptions, it grew out of the water and became an island!

Believe It or Not! If it weren't for underwater volcanoes, the Hawaiian Islands would not exist!

Millions of years ago, our moon was very busy with eruptions of its own! The dark spots on the surface tell a tale of ancient lava flows. Many other moons and planets have also had blasts in their pasts!

CHAPTER 5
TAKE COVER!

Volcanoes may be cool, but those awesome explosions come at a price. Hot ash from an eruption can **pollute** the air and hurt wildlife.

When magma moves inside of a volcano, rocks may also move to fill in the gaps. This can make the ground shake, which is called an **earthquake**.

A **landslide** is a large amount of soil and rock that slides down a slope very quickly. Volcanoes have gasses that break down rocks, causing landslides.

A **tsunami** is a massive ocean wave. A volcano can collapse into the sea during an eruption, making a fast and furious tsunami.

Believe *It* or *Not!* When it comes to sinking ships, cannonballs aren't the only culprits. Underwater volcanoes make gas bubbles that can change the **density** of the water, making ships sink!

Anak Krakatau

CHAPTER 6
FIERY FAME

If volcanoes "blow" your mind, here are some names you need to know!

In 1883, Krakatau erupted and collapsed, causing a terrible tsunami. Its explosion was so loud that it ruptured people's eardrums from 40 miles away! The volcano has grown back over time and is now called Anak Krakatau, or "Child of Krakatau."

Mount Vesuvius

The Mount Vesuvius eruption is no legend. In 79 AD, the city of Pompeii became an ash-covered graveyard.

The newest belief is that a 570-degree heat wave killed the victims instantly. Today, you can walk the amazing **ruins** of the city these people called home.

Believe It or Not! Out of the 20,000 people in Pompeii, around 2,000 chose to stay. The volcano's ashes fell so quickly that it preserved the shapes of their bodies. You can still see their lifelike poses, as if they are frozen in time.

May 18, 1980, was a day for the history books. After 123 years of rest, Mount Saint Helens woke up in a rage. It was the worst volcanic eruption the United States had ever seen.

Before an eruption 640,000 years ago, the Yellowstone Caldera was a supervolcano. A **caldera** is a volcano that has collapsed during an eruption. Magma is still brewing below this beast, and experts are sure it will erupt again.

Whether creating new islands or destroying old cities, volcanoes have made their marks on history. As we continue to study the world's volcanoes, our newest discoveries leave us "bursting" with excitement!

GLOSSARY

caldera: a crater formed by a volcano that has collapsed or exploded.

density: the amount of mass an object has compared to how much space it takes up.

earthquake: when the ground shakes.

landslide: a large amount of soil and rock that slides down a slope very quickly.

lava: magma that has reached the earth's surface.

magma: hot, melted rock below the earth's surface.

magnitude: the level of a volcano's eruption on the Volcano Explosivity Index (VEI).

pollute: to make dirty and unhealthy to live in.

ruins: what's left behind after disaster has struck.

supervolcanoes: the most destructive type of volcano.

tsunami: a massive ocean wave caused by a sudden displacement of water.

volcanologist: a scientist who studies volcanoes.

Ripley® Readers

Ready for More?

Ripley Readers feature unbelievable but true facts and stories!

LEVEL ONE — *Sounding it out*

LEVEL TWO — *Reading with help*

LEVEL THREE — *Independent reading*

LEVEL FOUR — *Chapters*

Baby Animals!

Bugs!

Dogs with Jobs

Shipwrecks

Sports!

Trains!

Roller Coasters

Mummies

For more information about Ripley's Believe It or Not!, go to www.ripleys.com